Depression

Hope for a Hard Season

Christine M. Chappell

newgrowthpress.com

New Growth Press, Greensboro, NC 27401
newgrowthpress.com
Copyright © 2024 by Christine M. Chappell

All rights reserved. No part of this publication may be reproduced, stored in a retrieval system, or transmitted in any form by any means, electronic, mechanical, photocopy, recording, or otherwise, without the prior permission of the publisher, except as provided by USA copyright law.

Unless otherwise noted, Scripture quotations are from The ESV® Bible (The Holy Bible, English Standard Version®). ESV® Text Edition: 2016. Copyright © 2001 by Crossway, a publishing ministry of Good News Publishers. The ESV® text has been reproduced in cooperation with and by permission of Good News Publishers. Unauthorized reproduction of this publication is prohibited. All rights reserved.

Scripture quotations marked NLT are taken from The *Holy Bible*, New Living Translation, copyright © 1996, 2004, 2015 by Tyndale House Foundation. Used by permission of Tyndale House Publishers, Inc., Carol Stream, Illinois 60188. All rights reserved.

Scripture quotations marked NIV are taken from THE HOLY BIBLE, NEW INTERNATIONAL VERSION®, NIV® Copyright © 1973, 1978, 1984, 2011 by Biblica, Inc.® Used by permission. All rights reserved worldwide.

Cover Design: Dan Stelzer
Interior Typesetting/eBook: Lisa Parnell, lparnellbookservices.com

ISBN: 978-1-64507-435-9 (Print)
ISBN: 978-1-64507-436-6 (eBook)

Library of Congress Cataloging-in-Publication Data on file

Printed in India

31 30 29 28 27 26 25 24   1 2 3 4 5

While the labor and delivery of our third child was the quickest, the season that followed her arrival was by far the darkest postpartum period I have ever experienced. Don't get me wrong—I absolutely loved my daughter. But never before had I battled against such indifference to my newborn baby. Never before had I felt so *unlike* a doting mother. There seemed to be a growing disconnect between us that was worsened by the guilt I felt in forcing myself to care.

At my six-week postpartum checkup, it became clear that I was suffering something more than "baby blues." I told the doctor about my perplexing, unexplainable sadness. I shared about the lingering indifference I felt toward my baby and the distressing thoughts I had about harming myself. I didn't know what was going on or what I could do to feel "normal" again—but I knew what I was going through was too serious to keep secret. My doctor agreed and diagnosed me with postpartum depression.

WebMD defines postpartum depression as "a complex mix of physical, emotional, and behavioral changes that happen in some women after giving birth. According to the *DSM-5*, a manual used to diagnose mental disorders, PPD is a form of major depression that begins within 4 weeks after delivery. The diagnosis of postpartum depression is based not only on the length of time between delivery and onset but on the severity of the depression."[1]

While I wish I could say I walked away from that appointment with a fresh sense of hope, I can't. All the doctor had given me was a prescription—one I was reluctant to take. I wasn't offered any life-giving spiritual comforts. No practical counsel for how to take care of myself physically. No instruction on how to engage my fluctuating emotions while waiting for the deadening darkness to lift. No insight on what to do with the ticker tape of negative thoughts that plagued me.

Can you relate to my story in some way? Perhaps you crave the same meaningful comfort and practical counsel I yearned for those years ago. Whether you've been officially diagnosed with postpartum depression or you're simply a mother who's struggling during this overwhelming and exhausting season, my goal is that the following words would offer you the realistic hope you hunger for. This is a hard season, yet even here God's guiding hand will hold you fast (Psalm 139:10).

Your Unidentified Needs

This unwanted, disruptive affliction may have you feeling desperate for answers. Will investing in a quality set of earplugs or vitamin supplements immediately help you? Will eating more balanced meals and engaging in regular exercise lift the fog? How about more frequent date nights or afternoon naps? Can doctors or counselors offer you remedies or strategies for fast relief from what is overwhelming you?

Perhaps you are additionally discouraged because a remedy that worked well for another mom doesn't seem to be helping you. Do you wonder if you just need to muster up more faith to plow through this postpartum season? Should you sit tight and try to wait it out?

It's not unwise to ask these kinds of legitimate questions. We want to pursue godly means of alleviating suffering when it's within our ability to do so. But when depression care requires more individual nuance than one-size-fits-all or fix-it-fast solutions can offer, it can feel both defeating and discouraging. Sometimes maternal despondency endures in spite of doing everything we've been told to try. If it does, we may start to think we're a hopeless case—broken beyond repair.

So maybe you don't know all that is needed to assuage your melancholy today (I don't presume to have all the answers either!). But thankfully your condition is neither a surprise nor a mystery to your Maker. He knows how to turn the darkness before you into light and the rough places into level ground (Isaiah 42:16). More than that, he's promised to accomplish his redemptive work in your life. Though his timing and methods may look much different from what you would expect or prefer, take courage by choosing to lean onto *his* understanding in the days ahead (Proverbs 3:5). God will not withhold anything necessary for preserving you through this hard yet momentary season (2 Corinthians 4:17).

The dark days of postpartum motherhood cannot thwart God's good plan for your life (Job 42:2; Jeremiah 29:11).

Your View of Self and the World

It's easy to lose sight of all that you are in this postpartum period. Perhaps you view yourself as *only* a big, bundled mess of unruly emotions or *only* a body and brain that's gone haywire. Or perhaps the *only* lens you see yourself through today magnifies your sin struggles and spiritual doubts. The problem with these overly narrow views is that they don't reflect the complexity of your whole personhood, let alone your surrounding environment.

God created you as a moral being with dual natures: body (material) and spirit (immaterial). This means that postpartum depression always involves both your physical and spiritual being. A narrow focus on only one portion of your personhood is detrimental. *All of you* needs nurturing. *All of you* is facing this trial. *All of you* is being made to navigate circumstances beyond your control. Let's build a more robust view to demonstrate what I mean.

At the very center of your experience of despondency sits a crushed spirit, with your physical nature bearing down firmly on it. But as we zoom out from your embodied turmoil, we may also find relational or financial strains weighing heavily on you. The sorrow, anger, and performance pressure you might feel may keep tears close to the surface. Health concerns—real or imagined—may harass you, along with other distressing thoughts. You may vacillate between restlessness and resignation. The mundane demands of motherhood may interfere with other roles, responsibilities, and ambitions you highly value. Failed expectations may fuel disappointment or resentment. And if that's not enough, the unseen "powers of this dark world" (Ephesians 6:12) are doing what they can to rob you of hope—anything to convince you that the fight for faith is futile. Yet in all of this, the Lord is providentially ruling over your whole person and world, accomplishing his good purposes and building his eternal kingdom.

This description may not resonate with you entirely, but it suggests a fuller picture of you and your world than any oversimplified view can capture. So how might you, as a whole person, wisely engage all the challenges you're facing? In the coming sections, we'll briefly consider biblical comfort and counsel for the core facets of your material and immaterial self:

- *Your exhausted body* as it responds to physiological changes and stressors.
- *Your overwhelming emotions* as your moods swing from one extreme to another.
- *Your troubled mind* as you think about yourself and failed personal expectations.
- *Your burdened spirit* as you wrestle with faith-related doubts and questions.

As we reflect on these points, it's important that we do so with humility. Gray area exists. We must leave room for the mysterious interplay between your body and spirit as it exists in a world under God's providence. As a whole "wonderfully complex" person (Psalm 139:14 NLT), it is *by design* that complete self-knowledge is impossible for you. This means that it is not God's goal for you today to discover all the factors contributing to your experience of depression. You're not merely a puzzle—you're a mother whose fears the Father wants to calm with his love (Zephaniah 3:17).

Until more personal clarity comes, let's focus on what you *can* know while trusting God with all that's veiled (Deuteronomy 29:29).

Your Exhausted Body

What can adequately be said about the bodily toll motherhood has taken on you? Words like *fatigue*, *exhaustion*, and *weariness* are insufficient. Your tireless expenditures of energy paired with your physical limitations can sometimes seem like cruel providences—it's as if you're breaking down as life's demands are piling up! I remember suffering painful infections and uncomfortable birth-related wounds that would not properly heal. For a time, it felt like my entire body was going haywire. Yet, in the midst of that physical pain and weakness, there was still work to do—young children and pets to care for. Relational tensions and financial burdens to navigate. Life didn't stop just because I felt "as good as dead . . . with no strength left" (Psalm 88:4 NLT).

Can you relate? Do you feel like you're physically incapable of doing all that daily life seems to require of you? Are you reeling from birth-related surgery, injury, or complication? Struggling to breastfeed successfully or comfortably? Are you barely surviving on a negligible amount of sleep? Does it seem like your strength is breaking down while the demands of life keep piling up? If so, I want to acknowledge how difficult and disorienting this kind of pressure can be. It's not an imaginary affliction—it's the actual cost of mothering under the curse (Genesis 3:16).

Feeling physically overtaken on your postpartum journey is common and largely unavoidable. That's because on this side of heaven, we're fallen, fragile, and easily frustrated creatures. But while God didn't design us to suffer any kind of brokenness, he *did* always intend for us to be weak in ourselves and thus reliant on him for everything we need—physical power included. These realities are important to remember as we think biblically about postpartum perseverance. They give us wisdom for the next steps by adjusting our expectations and deepening our dependence.

Bodily strength is a gift to be stewarded by us, not sourced within us. It's true that you are created in God's image (Genesis 1:26), but sister, you're not made to be omnipotent or omnipresent like he is. God has not assigned to you those capabilities nor placed on you those expectations. Do you believe that weakness—not strength—is your natural default? That limitation is your inherent human nature? You cannot escape the fact that you were created from dust to be dependent. You do not uphold your world by your own power. Strength finds its origins in the Almighty alone: "For in him we live and move and exist" (Acts 17:28 NLT). Rest assured that your present physical capacities are under your Lord's sovereign control, with his focused attention. God knows the multifaceted pressures you face, and he has a plan to sustain you through them.

Reframing how we think about the ultimate source of our physical power frees us to reshape the expectations we have for ourselves during this hard season of motherhood. It's not that you *should* be able to manage your world but you *can't*; you were never meant to be sovereign or self-sufficient in the first place. Therefore, your task in this season is not to achieve supermom status—it's to live for God within the bodily boundaries he's given you. The goal is to be faithful with the energy you have been given to work with, however much or little that is.

How might embracing such a goal inform the decisions you make today?

As a child, I remember watching my mother as she learned to live with a debilitating back injury. In an effort to help manage the pain, my dad encouraged my mom to live as though she had a limited number of "strength chips" to draw from each day.

Naturally, the more strenuous physical activities were to be regarded as the most costly. Her back hurt most on the days when she overspent her daily chip limit, and it hurt least on days when she was more selective with what she gave her physical effort to. My dad's chip system not only reminded my mom to live wisely within her limits, but that she would surely suffer on the days when she overestimated her capabilities.

There's wisdom in living like you have limits—because you *do*.

Like my mom, you too are learning a new way to live in this season of motherhood. This calling has brought a fresh set of limitations and pressures—depression included. While you may not have predicted the physical demands of postpartum life, you can ask God to help you rightly prioritize your spending of the daily "strength chips" he gives:

> *Show me how to live within these bodily limits, Lord. Reveal to me the nonessentials I need to set aside in this season. Help me to discern how to best steward the strength you grant to me today. Give me faith to turn away from self-reliance and toward humble, courageous dependence. Embolden me to ask for help from others more quickly and frequently. Lord, you say that your grace is sufficient in my weakness. Would you teach me how to rest in that promise while I do what I can, one breath at a time? In Christ's name, amen.*

Your Overwhelming Emotions

Part of what you know for certain is the emotional intensity of the season you're in. This is hard. You are afflicted. Energy is low and demands are high. Your patience is thin, and your moods are fluctuating. You're reeling from dashed hopes and discouragement—there's hurt and disappointment in your heart. But sister, be encouraged: It's possible to *feel* like you are falling apart even though Christ holds you together (Colossians 1:17). Jesus will continue to bear you up even if you keep breaking down (Psalm 68:19). The Lord's presence will help you bridge the gap between your emotional pains and his eternal promises.

Postpartum depression has not loosened God's grip on you.

As you learn a new way of life in this season, you will also learn how to navigate sudden mood shifts on your postpartum journey. And this does not include the need for emotional avoidance or suppression. There is a way to "worship in spirit and truth" (John 4:24) as you engage the Lord with your authentic feelings. There is no need to get better at faking "fine!" Instead, your part is to bring your mangled moods to Jesus in prayer. His part is to pick apart the tangles by his Spirit and Word (Hebrews 4:12).

God is neither impressed by facades nor honored by disingenuous platitudes (Matthew 15:8). He knows which feelings you're tempted to edit out or not express to him (Psalm 139:4). Still, he has mercy to give those who cry out to him in their meltdowns—and his mercy is the sustaining grace you need in those moments (Hebrews 4:16). He bids you to come and take refuge in him, whatever your mood. Since your struggles pain your Savior's heart, you can be honest with him about the pain in yours (Isaiah 63:9).

- Feeling hopeless? Talk to Jesus about your despair.
- Feeling weary? Talk to Jesus about your discouragement.
- Feeling sad? Talk to Jesus about your grief.
- Feeling angry? Talk to Jesus about your complaint.
- Feeling anxious? Talk to Jesus about your fears.
- Feeling ashamed? Talk to Jesus about your stains.
- Feeling lonely? Talk to Jesus about your longings.
- Feeling apathetic? Talk to Jesus about your indifference.
- Don't know how you feel? Talk to Jesus about your confusion.

Dear sister, remember that your mood swings cannot overwhelm God's mercy (Lamentations 3:22–23). Remember that by faith he makes you a *new* creation, not an *impervious* one (2 Corinthians 5:17). Remember that in Christ you're a saint who still mothers in a body that is subject to death (Romans 7:24). Remember that your faithfulness does not look like personal perfection, but rather progression on a journey with Christ to become more like him (John 15:4, 2 Corinthians 3:18). Even when your emotions swing swiftly, God's love for you remains steady and sure (Romans 8:38–39). Turn toward the Lord and talk to him in those overwhelming moments—he is a refuge for you (Psalm 62:8).

One courageous step you can take today is to openly share your feelings with Jesus in prayer. Another step would be to share those feelings with someone else. This could be a family member, friend, mentor, or counselor—anyone you can trust to handle your emotional fragility with humility and compassion. Admittedly, such a step may feel even harder to take. You may feel shame at the prospect of being vulnerable in this way. Yet even Jesus admitted his suffocating grief and asked his friends for support: "My soul is overwhelmed with sorrow to the point of death. Stay here and keep watch with me" (Matthew 26:38 NIV). It's Christlike to engage others when you feel overwhelmed by emotion. Start with engaging God, and then ask for his help in determining the next person to talk to.

Father, I'm a mangled mess of emotion today. I'm sick and tired of being so easily overwhelmed by sudden mood swings. As I pour out my heart before you, please comfort me with the promise of your presence. Help me to remember that my instability is not my identity. Have mercy on me in my meltdown moments. Deepen my confidence to talk to you about my distress and grant me courage to talk to others about it as well. Would you bring me someone I can entrust my feelings to—someone who can counsel me according to your Word? Thank you, Lord, for hearing my cries. In Jesus's name, amen.

Your Troubled Mind

When my nine-year-old daughter learned I was working on a resource for moms who are feeling sad after having a baby, a look of curious confusion came over her face. She inquired, "Why would a mom feel sad after having a baby? Isn't that something to be happy about?"

My daughter's innocent questions took me back to the hard season I endured after *her* birth—they sounded like the thoughts I was wrestling with at the time. I didn't want to be bogged down by sadness and limitation. I thought I should have been joyful, capable, and productive. On the days I was irritable, discouraged, and apathetic, I condemned myself as a failure. Shouldn't I be able to "enjoy this season" like well-wishers exhorted me? Why was that so hard for me to do yet so easy for them to say?

I especially didn't think a born-again mother was supposed to feel *depressed*. I thought I should feel blessed. I should enjoy this newborn season. I thought I *shouldn't* be sad or angry or harboring resentment toward my husband and children. I thought I *shouldn't* be fazed by hurt and heartbreak—or want to quit life in the wake of it.

But my responses to layered postpartum pressures did not align with my expectations. Worse yet, they didn't align with others' expectations of me. Unkind words of rebuke from a few people in my life added to the shame I already felt. It was as if I was failing myself and my family and God as well.

When you think about the expectations you have for yourself as a mother, what rules come to mind? Does a checklist of "should" or "shouldn't" overwhelm your heart to the point of despair? Has personal introspection morphed into morbid obsession as you have tirelessly tried to solve the depression puzzle? Do you think that if you could just be a stronger, healthier, more capable mother, you wouldn't be such a burden or embarrassment? Do you fantasize about being a different woman or living a different life?

As you think about your unmet personal expectations, I want to caution you against a perfectionistic attitude—it will only keep you stuck in despair and anxiety. How can you tell if this mindset is adding to your mental misery? Watch out for these types of gospel-less thoughts:

- Either I'm always pleasant or I'm a hypocritical Christian.
- Either I'm absolutely perfect or absolutely pitiful.
- Either I never groan or God is disappointed in me.
- Either I "keep calm and carry on" or I'm not a real Christian.
- Either I get my mood swings in check or I'll lose God's favor.
- Either I'm always strong and steady or I'm a terrible excuse for a mother.
- Either I figure out how to be free of depression or my life is not worth living.

Does this merciless tone undergird the way you think about yourself and your struggles? If so, it's critical for you to understand that God is not pressuring you to be a perfect mother—as if you could be! While this postpartum journey may feel more like a sentence of death than something precious to savor, it's a lie that faithful moms should never feel "crushed and overwhelmed beyond [their] ability to endure" (2 Corinthians 1:8 NLT). It's also a lie that you must live as a slave to your own expectations. You're called to live by the light burden of Christ's commandments (Matthew 22:36–40, 1 John 5:3)—not the crushing "shalls" or "shall nots" you impose on yourself.

One way to productively explore punishing thought patterns is to write down your expectations. List the unspoken "shoulds" and "shouldn'ts" that bind your mind. From your present perspective, list the "always" and "never" statements that characterize a good mother. Here are a few examples:

- I *shouldn't* be sad and struggling to function.
- I *should* be strong and capable.
- A good mom is *always* calm and collected.
- A good mom *never* asks for help.

Take a few days to work on building this list. Give yourself space to keep a running tab on the thoughts you notice that fit into this pattern. Then, with the help of a trusted friend, mentor, or counselor, differentiate the life-draining, self-made laws you are trying to keep from the life-giving commandment to "love the Lord your God with all your heart and with all your soul and with all your mind" (Matthew 22:37). How do the Scriptures interact with your list? Do your expectations align with what God has told you is most important? Remember the exhortation from Micah: "He has told you, O [mother], what is good; and what does the Lord require of you but to do justice, and to love kindness, and to walk humbly with your God?" (6:8).

Sister, you're accountable to only one Lawgiver (1 Corinthians 4:3–4). This is really good news for you today! God knows you cannot live up to your own standards, let alone his exceedingly higher ones

(Exodus 20:1–17). That is why he sent Jesus to be your Savior—the obedient law-keeper and spotless sacrifice you need to be approved in God's sight (2 Corinthians 5:21). You cannot earn "garments of salvation" by being a good mom any more than you can lose Christ's "robe of righteousness" by being a depressed mom (Isaiah 61:10). Dwell on the grace Christ was crucified to give you. He set you free from the burden of being perfect (Romans 8:1–2).

Thank you that your thoughts toward me are never full of criticism and condemnation, Lord, but instead are always full of love and kindness. How easily I slip into merciless self-talk when I fall short of my ideals. Lord, help me embrace the mind of Christ in these moments so that I might be transformed by beholding your glory and receiving your grace. Empower me to lay aside my personal expectations and live instead by your greatest command. By your Spirit, turn my inward focus outward and upward. Show me fresh ways to be a blessing to someone today while I wait for this darkness to lift. In Christ's name, amen.

Your Burdened Spirit

Let's face it: postpartum life is not typically defined as a season of order! Rather, loud noises often abound with a newborn in the home. Living daily in survival mode may mean that chores go undone and showers go untaken, dishes pile high in and around the kitchen sink, and laundry litters the floor as if a domestic tornado has ripped through the room. For some mothers, intensifying relational conflicts bring an additional disruption to peace in the home—spouses may argue over responsibilities and older children may lash out in response to the presence of a new sibling.

Does it feel like your whole world is in disordered upheaval?

It's normal to experience faith-related doubts and questions when life seems out of control. You may wonder what God is up to. You might wonder why he's let you experience hurt and heartbreak. Are you suffering because he's disappointed or angry? Does he plan to redeem your pain and restore your joy? Has he abandoned you?

The trouble with faith-related questions and doubts is not having them but being hesitant to explore them. It may seem unfaithful to confess such deep concerns, but Scripture teaches that wrestling with this kind of trouble is a critical step toward our spirit's unburdening. To experience Christ's comfort in this season, you'll need to practice examining your doubts.

In Psalm 77, we observe a burdened spirit that you can likely relate to. His days are troubled. His nights are sleepless. He struggles to pray. He's grown weary of crying out to God for help. Past flourishing makes his present withering all the more painful.

When he thinks about God, his distress actually *increases*. Yet, he realizes the revival he needs won't come through hopeless resignation. So he pivots from dwelling on despair to making a "diligent search" (v. 6). In doing so, he gives voice to some of the most important questions a person could ask in their affliction:

> Has the Lord rejected me forever? Will he never again be kind to me? Is his unfailing love gone forever? Have his promises permanently failed? Has God forgotten to be gracious? Has he slammed the door on his compassion? (Psalm 77:7–9 NLT)

Do these difficult questions reflect some of your own? If so, take comfort that they find their origins in the inspired Word of God. The psalmist's confusion is embedded into the songbook of God's people for our endurance and encouragement (Romans 15:4). This kind of spiritual grappling was corporately acknowledged and regularly sung about in Jewish congregations. Jesus himself would have lifted his voice to this lament! We simply cannot conclude that it's unfaithful to ask questions like these. We go wrong in our unwillingness to engage them with gospel truth, or in the futile attempt to locate their answers within our circumstances.

Sister, you can't know all God is doing in your disordered world today, but you can know that depression will tempt you to focus more on the *existence* of doubt than the *examination* of it. As long as your questions about God and his promises persist, the comfort of your spirit will remain elusive. That's why of all the places to surrender in postpartum motherhood, the arena of doubt is *not* one of them.

Today you can start to unburden your spirit by making a list of your faith-related questions. Then, with the help of a Spirit-filled friend or counselor, commit to making a diligent search. Let the Scriptures examine your doubts. Let your spirit wrestle *for* God. The comfort you crave will come no other way.

> *Lord, I confess that my spirit is burdened with questions and doubts. I don't know what to make of my confusion. What I know to be true about you doesn't seem to align with my circumstances. Would you lead me by your Spirit and Word as I start to doubt my doubts? Show me where I believe lies and heal my unbelief. Forgive me where I have drawn wrong conclusions about your character. Help me to better understand who you say you are and what you promise to do. Grant me a gracious helper who can support me as I seek to experience your comfort. In Jesus's name, I pray. Amen.*

Your Ultimate Hope

Faith-related doubts don't have to lead to disillusionment in postpartum depression. When engaged with the Scriptures, they can lead us toward realistic hope. For example, consider the questions we just read from Psalm 77. What comfort did this man's search yield? His reflections turned his focus away from his present fears and toward God's past faithfulness. He placed his distressing chapter into God's larger story of deliverance. He remembered that the Almighty uses his power to redeem his people, not destroy them (v. 14–15); that God's ways carve *through* great waters, not around them (v. 19). He remembered that the Lord's presence is not always perceived but is always with us (v. 19) and that God is like a good shepherd who leads his "people like a flock" (v. 20).

The same comforts welcomed by the psalmist long ago are for you. You have a Redeemer, and this means God isn't expecting you to be a supermom or to deliver yourself from postpartum depression. Instead, the Lord expects you to be a work in progress until he finishes his work in you (2 Corinthians 3:17–18; Philippians 1:6). Until then, God will be faithful to lead through the deep waters (Isaiah 43:2). Take courage: you are traveling in a glorious direction (2 Corinthians 4:17). You are not stuck in permanent overwhelm and exhaustion. God won't leave you here forever.

There will be times when you won't perceive God's presence—you'll have to "walk by faith, not by sight" (2 Corinthians 5:7). But the God who died for you cannot lie to you—he's with you always, just as he promised, no matter how you feel

(Numbers 23:19, Matthew 28:20). Remember that Jesus is *your* Good Shepherd—you belong to his flock. He's leading you through great waters to green pastures (Psalm 23:2–3). Restoration lies ahead. Resurrected life awaits. Your Shepherd has something better in mind than "back to normal" for you—he's making you like himself. He's making you *new*.

Seasons change, dear sister. And by God's grace, you will too (Romans 8:29). This is your ultimate hope in postpartum depression: in Christ, your story does not end in darkness and death, but light and life.

> And I will lead the blind in a way that they do not know, in paths that they have not known I will guide them. I will turn the darkness before them into light, the rough places into level ground. These are the things I do, and I do not forsake them. (Isaiah 42:16)

Endnote

1. Debra Fulghum Bruce, "Postpartum Depression," WebMD, August 23, 2022, https://www.webmd.com/depression/postpartum-depression.